Contents

Words appearing in the text in bold, **like this**, are explained in the Glossary.

 Find out more about India at
www.heinemannexplore.co.uk

Where is India?

To learn about India we meet three children who live there. India is a huge country. It is in Asia. Many people live in India.

▼ This is a map of India. The capital of India is Delhi.

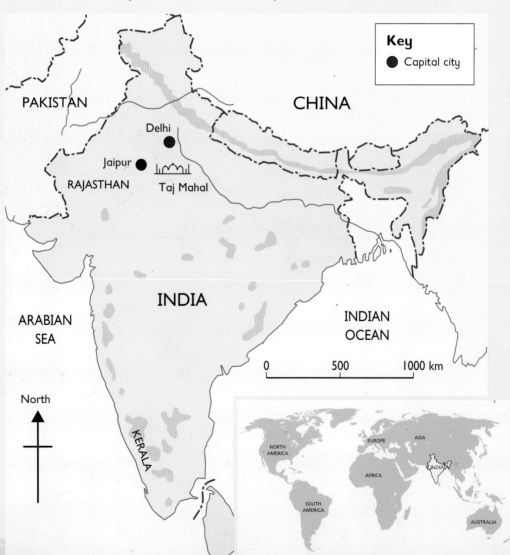

www.heinemann.co.uk/library
Visit our website to find out more information about **Heinemann Library** books.

To order:
 Phone 44 (0) 1865 888066
 Send a fax to 44 (0) 1865 314091
💻 Visit the Heinemann Bookshop at www.heinemann.co.uk/library to browse our catalogue and order online.

First published in Great Britain by Heinemann Library, Halley Court, Jordan Hill, Oxford OX2 8EJ, part of Harcourt Education.
Heinemann is a registered trademark of Harcourt Education Ltd.

Editorial: Jilly Attwood, Kate Bellamy and Catherine Williams
Design: Ron Kamen and Celia Jones
Photographer: Rob Bowden/EASI-Images
Picture Research: Maria Joannou
Production: Séverine Ribierre

Originated by Ambassador Litho Ltd
Printed and bound in China by South China Printing Company

ISBN 0 431 11933 3 (hardback)
09 08 07 06 05
10 9 8 7 6 5 4 3 2 1

ISBN 0 431 11940 6 (paperback)
10 09 08 07 06
10 9 8 7 6 5 4 3 2 1

British Library Cataloguing in Publication Data

Parker, Victoria
We're From India
954'. 053

A full catalogue record for this book is available from the British Library.

Acknowledgements
Rob Bowden/EASI-Images pp. 1, 5, 6, 7, 8, 9, 10a, 10b, 11, 12, 14, 15a, 15b, 16a, 16b, 17, 18, 19a, 19b, 20, 21a, 21b, 22, 23a, 23b, 24, 25, 26, 27, 28a, 28b ; Corbis/Royalty Free pp. 4a, 4b, 30c; Getty Images/Photodisc pp. 13, 29, 30b.

Cover photograph of Choti and her friends, reproduced with permission of Rob Bowden/EASI-Images.

Many thanks to Choti, Surya, Subodh and their families.

Every effort has been made to contact copyright holders of any material reproduced in this book. Any omissions will be rectified in subsequent printings if notice is given to the publishers.

The paper used to print this book comes from sustainable resources.

India has snowy mountains, sandy beaches, steamy jungles, dry **deserts** and wet **plains**.

Meet Choti

Choti is seven years old. She lives with her mother and father, three brothers, two sisters, two aunts and four cousins.

Choti's father

Choti

Choti's mother

▲ Choti's house does not have electricity or running water.

◄ Choti's loose shirt and trousers are called *shalwar kameez*.

Choti lives in Rajasthan. This is a very hot, dry part of India. Choti wears **traditional**, light clothes to keep cool.

On the farm

Choti's family have a small farm. They grow wheat and vegetables to eat and sell.

▲ Choti's family use oxen to **plough** the land.

▲ Choti's mother is milking the buffalo.

Choti's family are **vegetarian**. This means they do not eat meat. The family keep a few chickens for eggs and a buffalo for milk.

Choti's day

Choti goes to school six days a week, from ten until five. She also has lots of jobs to do at home. She gathers firewood for cooking and collects water from the village **well**.

▼ Water from the well is used for drinking, cooking and washing.

Choti is learning how to **embroider** bright material. Her mother and the other village women sell their beautiful material in markets and shops.

India's history

Many of India's cities were built hundreds of years ago. This is Jaipur. It is a very old city in Rajasthan.

Over the years, India has been ruled by lots of rich, powerful people. They made many beautiful buildings, which people from all over the world come to see today.

▲ This famous palace is called the Taj Mahal.

Meet Surya

This is Surya. She is seven years old. Surya comes from Kerala, where it is hot and rainy.

Surya's mother

Surya's father

Surya

Saranya

Surya lives with ▶ her mother and father, her sister and her grandmother.

Surya lives in a house on a huge tea **plantation**. Her father works in the tea company's office.

▲ Surya is friends with the other children who live on the tea plantation.

At school

Surya goes to school six days a week, from half past eight until four o'clock. She travels there by bus. There are 40 children in Surya's class.

Surya has all her lessons in Hindi and English. Hindi is the official language of India. Surya is also learning the state language of Kerala.

Work and play

Surya's family have a garden where they grow fruit, vegetables and flowers. It is Surya's job to water the plants.

In the evenings, Surya has homework to do. Afterwards, she reads, paints, listens to music or plays with her friends. They enjoy board games and splashing about in a nearby stream.

Indian food

In many Indian families, the women get together to cook. A popular meal is vegetables cooked in spicy sauces and served with rice.

▲ In Surya's family, her grandmother, mother and sister cook together.

Some Indian people eat sitting on the floor. Others take their meals at a table. **Traditionally**, people scoop up their food with their fingers or with pieces of flat bread.

Meet Subodh

Subodh is eight years old. He comes from a city called Mumbai. Subodh lives in a flat with his mother and father.

▼ Subodh's father is an **engineer**.

Subodh's father

Subodh's mother

Subodh

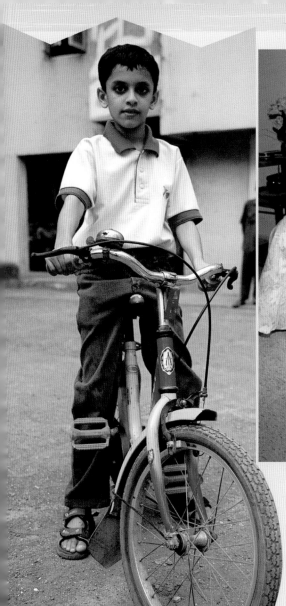

▲ Subodh's grandmother
is wearing a **sari**.

Subodh's grandparents live near by.
Subodh goes to visit them every day
after school. There is a yard where he
can ride his bike.

23

Living in the city

Subodh's family live in a large, modern city called Mumbai. The streets are full of people and traffic. It is very busy and noisy.

In Mumbai, there are lots of market
stalls, supermarkets and shops.
Subodh's family can buy all the things
they need here.

Family traditions

Subodh's family follow India's main religion, Hinduism. Subodh prays every day at a **shrine** in his home. He looks forward to **festivals**, such as **Divali**.

▲ Subodh's family think it is important to worship God.

harmonium

sitar

keyboard

▲ Subodh's mother is a music teacher.

Subodh enjoys playing musical instruments. He plays the electric keyboard. His mother plays the sitar and his father plays the harmonium.

27

Out and about in India

India is very big. People have to travel long distances to visit their families or holy places. Trains and buses are very popular because most people do not own a car.

▲ India has the second biggest railway system in the world.

There are many wildlife parks in India. These are home to animals that used to live in the wild. There are black bears, tigers, rhinoceroses, and lions.

Indian fact file

Flag	Capital city	Money
	Delhi	Rupee

Religion
- The main religion in India is Hinduism. There are also people who follow Islam, Christianity, Sikhism and Buddhism too.

Language
- India's official languages are Hindi and English. There are 15 other main languages spoken in different parts of the country.

Try speaking Hindi!
namaste .... hello
aap kaise hain? .... how are you?
shukriya .... thank you

Find out more about India at
www.heinemannexplore.co.uk

Glossary

desert very hot, dry area of land that has almost no rain and very few plants

Divali Hindu festival when people decorate their homes with candles and lanterns

electrical engineer someone who designs elcectrical equipment

embroider sew a pattern on to material using coloured threads

festival big celebration for a town or country

plain open area of flat, grassy land with few trees

plantation large area of land where crops, such as tea, are grown

plough to turn over the soil ready for planting

sari long piece of cloth wrapped around the waist and shoulders

shrine special place with a holy picture or object that people pray in front of

traditional the way things have been done for a long time

vegetarian someone who does not eat meat

well hole in the ground where people can get water

More books to read

Around the World: Schools, Margaret Hall (Heinemann Library, 2002)

Around the World: Transport, Margaret Hall (Heinemann Library, 2002)

We come from: India, David Cumming (Hodder and Stoughton 2002)

Index